ECO–DEMENTIA

MADE IN MICHIGAN WRITERS SERIES

General Editors

Michael Delp
Interlochen Center for the Arts

M. L. Liebler
Wayne State University

Advisory Editors

Melba Joyce Boyd
Wayne State University

Stuart Dybek
Western Michigan University

Kathleen Glynn

Jerry Herron
Wayne State University

Laura Kasischke
University of Michigan

Thomas Lynch

Frank Rashid
Marygrove College

Doug Stanton

Keith Taylor
University of Michigan

*A complete listing of the books in this series can
be found online at wsupress.wayne.edu*

ECO-
DEME
NTIA

Poems by Janet Kauffman

WAYNE STATE UNIVERSITY PRESS
DETROIT

ISBN 978-0-8143-4381-4 (paperback); ISBN 978-0-8143-4382-1 (ebook)

Library of Congress Control Number: 2017941839

Publication of this book was made possible by a generous gift from The Meijer Foundation.

Wayne State University Press
Leonard N. Simons Building
4809 Woodward Avenue
Detroit, Michigan 48201-1309

Visit us online at wsupress.wayne.edu

Poems in this collection, some in a slightly different version, appeared in the chapbook *oh corporeal*, and in *Calibanonline, Cream City Review, Guernica, Michigan Quarterly Review*, and *New American Writing* 32.

CONTENTS

1. ECO-DEMENTIA

2. UNDERCURRENT

3. THE KNIFE IN THE FISH

ECO–DEMENTIA

(def.) – ō-kō də **men**(t) əh(c̄)ə   condition of humanity;
a love of the living world while causing and suffering
its destruction.

from *Pollard's Synthetic Speller*

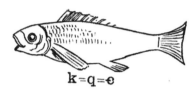

k = q = c

fern verse first verbs
jerk learn girl firms
born horse bore porch
sort thorn wore horns
pint drill twist splint
lint fill tilt fists
fob nod hot fog
sob Todd sot hog
rock cross thong bonds
lock moss song ponds
hooted hooded routed
rooted wooded counted
smoke mole grope notes
choke hole rope bones
led hen leg sex
fed men wet yes
he mere fee bleed
she sere free weed
tide time mire files
life line wire dives
jade cake page flame
wade rake wage snake

1

ECO–DEMENTIA

Before writing the large letters
of names of planets, or kinds of forks,
say a person tears a plant apart,
bloodroot, one word, and there is blood

or straps the wrinkled leaves of boneset
as bandage, as necessary, immersed.
A body in leaves, a body dressed,
four words, three words.

UNTIL THE FLOOD AND DOLLBABY
UNTIL THE FLOOD AND DOLLBABY

Until the flood and dollbaby
floats away she's hung up
in a snag one leg
making waves her webbed toes
an itty dam she's flotsam to be

as derelict we all go
unsalvageable
in the scheme of feast
to further feast
via much brilliance

bacterial or mandibular
the table set or cleared
the floor swept
we have so much to offer
let it be remembered

Practice for outside situations:

—This is a valley. This was a valley. This was a beautiful valley.

—The boy sits on the sidewalk. The man stands in the square. Birds fly to trees.

—Where is the governor's house? Where are pastures? Where are the rivulets?

—The footpath is steep. The river flows to a Great Lake. The bridge is narrow.

—The fish are green sunfish. The water is frozen. That plant is pokeweed.

—Where is Elm Street? Which are the elms? Where is Maple Grove?

—Please repeat that address. Did you say Route 12? Please repeat that address.

—Which mammals are hunted? Do you eat leaves of trees? May we rest here?

—The girl cuts a stalk. The wind blows at night. The siren is loud.

—What digs the large holes? Who opens the gate? Where are the berries?

—Pokeweed is poison. The gold moth is rare. The rock is conglomerate.

—We cross the stream. We have crossed the stream. We will cross the stream.

—Here is a burlap sack. There is a shell. This is a blue feather.

CAUGHT BETWEEN ROCKS

Caught between rocks, the blue
mud ushers in
glacial till.

Our feet are so old,
root hairs
in sand, the pace of plants,

god we are plodding,
sucking
and mouthing.

Leaves carve up air. Times
do change.
A new appendage, soaking

gauze, wire through the tongue.
Who can say
love, or drought, or name the place

we women are straddled, sodden,
at home
in so many bodies of water.

An elaboration of stalk
and stilts, Angelica leans,
she tilts, cantilevers

in chalk spray, the old bride
unhinged, stick arms magenta,
steampunk seed nails

click-clicking, horse-wheeling
there by the stream, hallelujah,
hallelujah, amen,

dug in now, dirty
as, yes, your hands.

DECAYING TO MORE

DECAYING TO MORE

Such are the symmetries,
you want to flail
and stir air like milk

contributing
to the mesh
the deer breath

wavering as well
with distant arrivals
of light

we are so close
even in half lives
touching

decaying to more
and more intimate
spaces

Every shot-through
winter scene crackles

from an edge, from memory.
Watch the old roots write.

Don't say what they're not,
those sticks at your feet,

a lie, a limit, the crimped
stalks of beech drops,

a scrawl diagrammed,
flower and all.

7

CUT THE LURE

CUT THE LURE

Cut the lure,
has it opened now,
your story?

Webs and dim branching,
cross-firing,
is someone there?

Floating under a bridge,
and on through,
was that the highpoint?

If he's on the road
when he falls asleep,
does light fade?

Just because one thing follows another
doesn't mean it does. In slow water
that leaf, the gold larvae may be clues,
but what about black and white cows
on swollen knees in the warehouse?
Jasper walks backwards, you've seen him
skate on ice the same way. Where is he now?
No answering at this time. Did fire fish tumble
under his blades? Questions cannot predict
a call from the Azores or from the sheriff
in Bad Axe in the Thumb. You've seen how
jewelweed snaps its seeds at a touch.

THE WHIRLWIND TIMES

Two caps on his head for the whirlwind times.
When one cap shears off, his ear bleeds.
Two shovels for hardpan and splintering,
laser trenchers for muck, dozers,
he has staunched the flow,
and earth-movers for, well,
moving earth.

Grass is cover, water is, rock is
a covering covering
boundless invisibles, black stuff and blue,
gold and green, he writes his wife,
and she writes, have you seen the great crested
flycatcher perched?
No, he says, but something.
A fragment, a shard
moving so fast, he says,
he couldn't tell.

The gnats with gray wings removed themselves to the bedroom and exhaled their sighs, counted the corners and angles, before packing it off to Panama. Didn't they know? We'd accompany them as they've accompanied us but there was no warning. The calm took two weeks to notice. Even now, there is fluttering some of the time. But they carried away the small shadows, that's verifiable. They took their good eyesight. The crooks of their legs. Every small thing we need.

ECO–DEMENTIA ECO–DEMENTIA

In this case he says take some time but I do believe time has taken us far too far for scattershot revelations or shortcuts through eco-dementia, for instance, and EF-4s in the cellar, where the crazy love of a slope takes over, that's all that's left, and the switchgrass outside, even the dirt, ends up in another county we don't know the name of or which way its waters flow.

WANTING ICE

Wanting ice
to be clear
over flowing water,
undisturbed
in spite of the usual
odds, slipping
under, among
bodies unshrouded,
to be visible
as painted turtles,
pumpkinseed or green
sunfish, the threatened
slippershell mussel,
to say it is
possible to tell
this from that.

INSTEAD OF FLYING IN WATER

INSTEAD OF FLYING IN WATER

Instead of flying in water, fish swim
and my mother wonders if they could
defy expectations. Just once.
Part the waters, take off and join
the old gang, schools of anabaptists
flying through sheds and airy quadrants—
their arms the arms of the great blue
heron, star-nosed mole, mottled sculpin—
as tyrants fall and before new ones
crop up, gut the sky, and claim all things
feather, skin, scale.

Quillworts half in
half out of the water,
their books would write us
veined and vascular too.
Warmwater, whatever
unannounced whiteout
blizzard hits our blood,
we're in for it,
two-thirds water,
even when iced
on a table, our own
name on the line.

KERATELLA OFFSHORE

Keratella offshore roto-tiffering around, a few cells
and cilia. And what's-his-name wants to gut
the EPA. Water is water, he says, maybe one or two
little things not quite right. But still. All it takes
is dredging say. Or the blue pond chemo cure,
he's seen that work.
Oh *Keratella*, please,
bloom red, balloon, show yourself,
whip-snap, weave complex paisley fabrics
from foot-glue, mix media on slow water,
raft the whole conglomeration into shore.
Make him say, I could do that art, that
suicide, sure, both of those things.

Referring to lowliest
lying sons of bitches
she says they're gone

they left fungi and tick
forgot carrion beetles
completely that's what

let them roll over easy
rub their bellies okay
just close their eyes

not one hairy spark
even long distance
not one more lick.

Two small legs, two small eggs.
Her small lies, her small eyes.

Every syllable is expressed
By one emission of the breath.

The four winds trumpet over dunes,
Over seven oceans and painted sky.

Step forward, yes, here are buttons of coral,
A scarab and blue beetle jewel.

Now take a daughter, whichever you choose,
Having previously leased these lands.

The largest quadrant shall be named first,
Followed by the next largest, and so on.

Need I waste time speaking of the art of weaving?
The management of pancakes and preserves?

Given the evidence of vase-painting girls,
They continue to amuse themselves in this way.

This is my desert daughter, do not deny her
Wishes, she will deliver herself as she must

From sickness, perils, drought, tedium.
A lithe stalk, she does not wither in such winds.

Zooplankton and more, those unreadable receipts at the bottom of a purse, in Pennsylvania they say pocketbook, and no you can't count invisibles in the green shallows, not from this stump, just worry those teeth up and down a bracelet, you can't go far into water or out without picking up sequins, cells, red smears of something defunct or intact, and like it or not, such jewelry is commonplace now, more worn than ever.

GLOSSED OVER

Glossed over, a sheen of ice clarifies
a gravel bed. We watch and don't lie down.

Winter sinks in. Ice plates stack and cantilever.
Every architecture

shatters sometime. See
the crinkle skirts, the music

dissolve to April and the small fish
Lampetra appendix, silver green,

augur somehow upwards
from the gravel bed. They pucker

sucker mouths and pick up
pebbles larger than their heads.

They set the stones, nest walls,
and twist that twist, complex

finger clusters flashing,
interlacing figure-eights.

We wear shoes and cotton socks,
and go so lovely slow slow slow in love

in counterpoise to silver glitter
water rippling inside rippling.

Air here
at the edge
small fires
one field sparrow
song
down-falling
no reason
to move

If you wake under cover of
deep undercover, under cloud-like mattressing blown in
from sweet-fruited floodplains,
you can see so damn clearly and crazy
a painted yellow circle, say,
sparking and spinning, one mayfly walking
the window, tracing the backslopes
of deer in the yard, there.

You're in between
earmuffing, milk-froth, the riot of utterly distancing
light years, dark, the warping of everything, see,
it's already slipping away, the sack
of the horrible, the disjoints and cursing,
fly-by-nights gone, the brain
is humming, something like blue feathers
stirring, unraveling, you know it
must be sun-rising.

And you wonder how the hell
will this kiss end?
Can a body hang on
to what dark is?

Your eyes are shut,
but the furnace clicks, you count to the flare,
and a wavering strumming collects off-site,
drawing as if you could see it, across November
and belly to belly, a semitropical line this morning.

Virtues enumerated add up
to wooziness every time,
notice the yawns
in a hayfield overblown
with bloom, the emerald
alfalfa, dew just off,
less than 30%
moisture after raking,
sun at 2 o'clock, a breeze,
nobody can even think
uprightness.

LANGUISH

LANGUISH

Speak to me in languish,
love, here where it rains
as much as suns, and water
flows to muck, blue-gray
marl. So slide, slow. You say,
we're in luck. Stuck.

UNDERCURRENT   2

They're able to live invisibly. Like Lazarus dead, but not absolutely, before Jesus wept and said, roll away the stone. You can see it, they live without limits. Fully functioning, with none of the usual obstacles.

When they pull a sheet, or reeds, over their bodies, they're gone. The space looks like a field, contoured, the soils striated, wavering in the heat. There's artistry, or subterfuge, in it. So much water-coloring, or drawing of chalk lines, pastel and charcoal, burnt sienna and beige, they're camouflaged even in bed, in plain sight.

And of course the same cloaking applies when they're out and about. Air settles on their shoulders, infiltrates their hair, and passersby notice nothing, maybe a shift in temperature, routine as that flow of cool on your arms from the dark of an alley.

No more than an undercurrent in daily life. In that way, they couldn't be more ordinary.

It's difficult to assess them morally. Do they kill animals for food? Or grow tubers and greens? Do they hurt each other in small ways, or worse? Do they seek justice for any reason?

Do they attend to the world at large? Or live wholly apart, the newsworthy world a nebulous swirl, not even a context for their unique situation, their struggles and passions.

One way or another, they're a pair, we might as well say *virtually*, as we say about so much these days that's out there somewhere we can't go with our own bulk and substance.

But still. They're more than that, we sense it, we have a suspicion. They are what they are – fully realized, and shameless.

They apparently do more than have sex, though that's the core of life. Imagine, unseen, with no schedule, how much time they lavish on the body, how they abandon restraint, and don't give a thought to anything but the expanses and apertures, ridiculous topographies, the startling landscape of inlets, protuberances, appendages. How the fingers play and the belly shudders.

They certainly entertain themselves, to the point of hazard, and have invented out of those recreations a system of marks, some call it a language, we have yet to decipher.

All of this comes to us remotely, like the digital images from the Mars Rover, out there rolling up and down the landscape, communicating with 0s and 1s, like letters, alchemic, making words we recognize, the red rocks in heaps, and the crusty sand. We presume they collide and orbit somehow, snapshots from Hubble, the collisions of spheres, catastrophic in glitter and neon, now placed in evidence.

The consequence of their connection, in other words, can be registered, envisioned. A look off to the side, or, for more precision, close your eyes completely, as you do when you wake, to set in memory the landslide you just dreamed, tall brick buildings slipping into a ravine.

An odd cut of intense color, a rock in sharp focus that blurs and flattens then returns to solid rock, a surge of cascading emotions, then calm – there's that. And touch. Alone in a grassland, you're aware of the hairs on your arm, something blowing, there.

If we knew their names, they'd no doubt be strings of vowels, spoken while breathing. Or the names would conjure other invisibles, remote and scurrilous, geographic couplings with no witnesses, Mount Kailash with Lake Manasarovar.

Some try to track their whereabouts, upheavals in the steppes of Kazakhstan, or that flow of fabrics and waters of Manhattan. Various underpinnings or overthrowings of modulated landscapes. Their blurrings and breathings.

They're best known by their refusals, and endless indulgences. Their nomadism. Their naked opposition to restraint. The way they suck down polluted waters and spit them back clean. We presume.

Even here. The Great Sulfur Pond in Lake Erie, a black hole in the lake on the old maps, has migrated onshore and bubbles up fabulous algal paints. Hundreds of egrets stroll the shore on black stilt legs and strike at fish. Legs and beaks flash above. Fin and flesh below.

3

THE KNIFE IN THE FISH

By the time you think weaponry,
the blood-script of tall grass,
which must have been quick
razor-cuts criss-crossing
your arms, red lines of A's
and X's and Y's, and for all that
so little pain, by the time you see
letters they're already erasing,
smeared, but it's very clear how
in this same world, another field,
a body blown to the ground
has already read every word.

A warring machine
flexes, exploding
bird song.
The wren
in the redbud.
Cataclysm
and chorus.
This place
or the other,
so many
lines drawn,
and not one is
nature
poetry.

Upended
by error and X-rays,
too much foliage,
crenelated,
dark at the root,
we're rolling again
downhill.

Noduled
landscapes, the ultra
scene
and that zero
tunnel, that's nothing,
she says,
the carotid.

It's the rest that matters,
as if a crash
IDs the sycamore
more than trunk,
limb, crown,
or the leaf so large
it covers a face.

THE KNIFE IN THE FISH
THE KNIFE IN THE FISH

The lion in the cloud, the scar in her palm, three birds on the mantle, a shoe in the gutter, wind in the basement, a tooth in the grass, green ice in blue water, her hair in the comb, the horse in the field, snow on the rug, the knife in his thigh, the knife on the board, the knife in the fish, dragonflies on the cake, the cake in the wagon, her foot on the pedal, the chair in the fire, the rock on the nest, the bleach in the baby, the house on the barn, the book in the coffin, the dog in the stream, the rope on the rail, a boy in a tree, the doll on a stick, the seed in the scat, the girl in the shed, a bowl on the floor.

HE'S SEEN IT CRAWL

A baby bottle floats by. A raft of branches. Someone says one thing after another, it has come to this. Again. Still, here isn't as bad as there. Water rolls the stone away, pea gravel clicks and walks, and twigs too, step upstream. Good legs, she says, on bugs.

The other way, towards the lake, in the rotunda, and the next one, and the next, cows circle, knees together. Somebody counts the merry-go-rounds inside, competing with tunes. He says even if the milkmaid goes outside with a pail, it doesn't help. Water slides, he says, he's seen it crawl.

Many small children have taken to hiding
along the stream. Or in swamps. They dive.
They disappear for months, any season.

It is not like skipping school. They study
water, muskrats. They collect wetland plants
and press them. There is always paper.

They are so poor they have little hair
and bare feet. There is never a trail
of crumbs or plastic or size 5 shoe-prints.

We miss them, but they have each other.
And something else. We're not sure
if they've made reed flutes or if they hum.

The blur of beginnings of branchings in winter, the horizon, the blur of a voice behind the wall, of mountain beyond mountain, the blur of the blast in granite, the pump pumping, the bomb hitting the bush in the desert, the blur of a hand slapping, the blur of Indiangrass in slight breeze, of late afternoon, of sledding at night downhill once in the quarry, of distance, of nearness, of now, the blur of landslide, of any sequence of thought, a sheet of paper, the blur of day to day.

UNCALLED-FOR

You can't predict the skeleton crew or day or year brown rain will wash. Unless you carve witch hazel in the old style, lesser than a nightstick, capped with sprouts of pig hair from the muck trail. Others say it takes no more than a piece of paper, an arrangement of uncalled-for words, pawpaw seeds on a string, a broken white cup, five stones.

Now with the tallest trees slashed, the long-legged Naiads appear in the willows, draped in fog. Look at their feet in sand, their waterweed hair. Their mouths are open, filled with spring water. Familiar animals approach. Not one speaks. Two branches clap two stones together and blue sparks fly. It's no surprise, you can see how it happens, dead leaves catch fire. And wet as they all are, and safe, trunk and limb, they lie down and roar and burn.

DODDER IS NO DAUGHTER

DODDER IS NO DAUGHTER

Driving isn't doddering but
what is? dodder is no daughter
either. We go on and on
a footpath by the stream
considering time allotted,
creatures lost, the planetary
devastation, before stumbling
into stinging nettles looped
with dodder, silly string, he says,
day-glo orange, flashy, splashy
sci-fi crazy bitty flowering.

The spores and tight-wads rooted, stuffed in wormholes and pipes, it makes you wonder who can reach water, cut loose the brown tissue paper, thank you, and cut out shirt patterns caps capes here's a bolt of brocade and foliage, it's spring, the vultures sweep over all this wasteland you used to call it before it took hold and dressed you.

BEFORE IT TOOK HOLD

The devil's walking stick he says
he found it in a scraped ditch
the trunk a stick a few stiff branches
covered with scimitar thorns only a devil
could have picked it and walked off
without tearing his own flesh
without cutting his wrists
without falling upon it
or with greater force in the forest
slicing the leaves or twirling it
like a blender grinding a path
through elderberries and laurel
without bloodying his feet
without shredding his own pajamas
without burying splinters in his eyes

Pull back the foil this is the sweetest
drink you can sip from the corner
he always asks for it bring that cup
it's syrup my mother says
no it is the sweetest drink
there's nothing like it try it
drink from this cup

THE SAME SPIKE DRIVEN OR PULLED

When they left the house the last thing
he did was pull the spike from the stump
where he speared ears of corn for squirrels.

Jesus suffered on the cross, his hands
and his feet, each one nailed through flesh
to wood, until he was brought down.

Suffering or release from suffering is
in my father's world
the same spike driven or pulled.

Through one gate then another the chain link
and concertina wire the blasted bass the horn
hits and flows through steel through cloth through skin

in the stress position in the ward some say "simulation"
or if they have joined in "hallucination"
or if they suffer it "pain unto death" unspoken

because nothing makes a sound not one of us
animals in the end behind walls even the air
drowned out mouths open in every cell

The horse in the circus in the yard has sharpened teeth
a black dog ran under the table at the apple tree
a man is a bird on the peak of the roof all day
three men with guns stand at the door at one o'clock

the man with bug eyes hovers over the bed
the man with bug eyes in the mirror has a knife
the man with bug eyes takes every shoe in the closet
a woman spins in a red skirt and explodes the trees

a banana is a turnip a handkerchief is a sock
which way is home do you have a car do you drive
take me to Mary Jane's the Water Gap Pop's farm
the coat has arms has legs has a hatchet

there's nothing there but green grass and sticks
the water is loud with frogs at the bench
brown needles lie on the path in the woods
I know where you live but I don't know who you are

The root the food of the underground but without digging into dark, just crush the hand of the leaf in your fingers and chew, strip the bark and suck, it will keep you going, he said, the stalk, the fibers, and don't stop walking, don't miss the cut-off out of here.

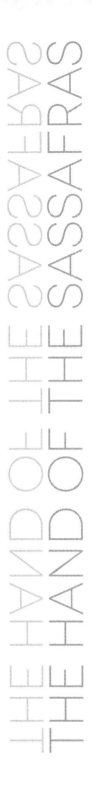

THE HAND OF THE SASSAFRAS

THE DRIFTING DOWN

THE DRIFTING DOWN

A hawk
tore the mourning dove
apart on the lamp post
he watched
the drifting down
feathery slow rain
yes it is still falling
take an umbrella he said
for your own protection

Xylem is the up pipe
he said, and also phloem
is love
or he said nothing indoors
reading eating packing

Love as love was not
possible it followed
the botanical
or chemical but couldn't precede
it wasn't personal

When he couldn't read
or eat or pack his things
he could say blood
feeds the heart
he could say vena cava.

If you eat what is offered you will sicken and your wounds
won't heal but will open up further the gashes on each side
purple when the bleeding stops it will blacken will ooze
and your hands will swell your ankles will swell
you'll be sitting in the same hard chair without light
week after week they will question you in a language
you don't understand they pretend you understand
they have tools they drill holes in your hands and
bring food that has the appearance of a small animal
or toy and you ask them one question did I order this?

From the discrete and first crimp
the serrated pinking cuts his body
he walks off to the last boggled
wiring the loose ends hanging
he kicks the footstool refuses to speak
even in the green shade the one corner
out of range not targeted but still
crawling with insects he can't eat

IN HIS ARMS

In his arms, his belongings falling, flailing, knots and sleeves, they take wing, he says they take off, even the calves in the dark gnawing his fingers lose weight, their bones hollow out, they puff in the night from the darkest barns, he says shoo shoo get out of here, this is no place for babies, and spared, their screaming stops, he goes into every factory at night and unlocks the cages, lifts filthy animals into his arms, they catch the air, the cows kick off, chicks and chickens in clouds, resurrected he said once long ago.

Engulfed
the interstices stuffed
brand new like a pig with an apple
cooked cranked
he says like everyone there
take me home
he packs every day there's
nowhere to go no where
is home the original brain?
that baby that old one
with time unstuck and open
fields and everything to be
not not to be
is there

OH, CORPOREAL

Gulleted cells open up, it could be dismay at unstoppable
liveliness, yawning and yawning, you could be twenty
but here is the axe coming down

oh, corporeal

eating the foul stuff shoved, but still inside
locomotion and flagellation, there's the vertical
electric wire, a blade, in the green green grass

open your hand

all of the tools retract, scrape, and it could be you wake
with no dreams of degradation or blown bits of straw
on your knees, suck this sponge they say, and that you can do.

In the aftermath of purple cress, the cut-out leaf and shell casings, splints the ice water saws right through, the blue ashes snap and uproot cohosh, white snakeroot, green enameled floors too, one wall flies out the window if they say so, and they do, they did turn things around, the sandbar upstream sprawls here now.

LONG KNIVES ARE SHELVED
LONG KNIVES ARE SHELVED

Dolled-up deer with white paint around their eyes, and muskrats in cattails swaying – evensong, evensong. Long knives are shelved, they cut air only. Fog somehow slides by. A boy walks home via coyote. And at sunset, a woman watches a dress flame in the swamp. On a stake. Two minks ditch and dive, voguing, round-about. Water whips. People upslope say water whippets, but that's for a laugh. They walk inside and turn the cameras off.

The way the breast of a tree rises, not that way under the skin but open, lightning-struck and gashed, a body walking in clothes, filaments, gauze cut and stitched, familiar scars like that one or this one in the palm of the hand gristled, or the sliced flesh of persimmon, or you-name-it on the landscape, gouged.

SOME INTERMITTENCY

Some intermittency, some scatter
of flake or sheen
is enough to require fiction.

Nothing lies beside or apart
but through and through
a word sift.

Hyphenated in the habitude
of slope-to-stream,
we slip together.

red cloth to cover
        the battered mountain
gauze
        for fields of corn

as well as hands
        on Lake Erie, blue-green toxins,
and muslin
        on fires blistering

difficult to shroud
        the miles across the face of the seas
the space
        to Mars, our visible scars

debris trails
        small particulates, leaf litter
a dry scatter
        and sound of snares

when words fail
        to materialize
clear water
        or airy ecosystems, or soothe with

the letter o
        especially
well then
        breath fails too

COMPOSED
COMPOSED

Composed

no more

but asunder and saturated

as with color

feel how that feels

boundaryless

molten and glowing

subsumed fancy-free

brokenness is becoming now

and again

Photo by Christine Hume

Janet Kauffman has published three collections of poetry and numerous books of fiction, including the award-winning book of short stories, *Places in the World a Woman Could Walk*, as well as the creative nonfiction collection, *Trespassing: Dirt Stories and Field Notes* (Wayne State University Press, 2008). She lives in Hudson, Michigan, where she restored wetlands on her farm, now protected as a natural area for ecological study.